T0194981

Whitestone Girls

finding joy in who you are.
right here. right now.

A HEARTS-OPEN,
HANDS-ON BIBLE STUDY FOR GIRLS.

Tanya L. Schulz

WESTBOW
PRESS®
A DIVISION OF THOMAS NELSON
& ZONDERVAN

WestBow Press books may be ordered through booksellers or by contacting:

WestBow Press
A Division of Thomas Nelson & Zondervan
1663 Liberty Drive
Bloomington, IN 47403
www.westbowpress.com
1 (866) 928-1240

ISBN: 978-1-9736-9167-9 (sc)
ISBN: 978-1-9736-9169-3 (hc)
ISBN: 978-1-9736-9168-6 (e)

Library of Congress Control Number: 2020908819

Print information available on the last page.

WestBow Press rev. date: 05/20/2020

Dedication...

For the original **Whitestone girls** - Julia, Gracie, Aislinn, Brynn and Cameran. You were crazy and insightful, loud and loving. My heart was touched by how you cared for each other and you will forever be 'my girls'.

For my **mom and dad,** who listened to every idea I had and encouraged me every step of the way. You inspired me and kept me grounded, reminding me often of the reason for writing this curriculum. Mom ... I have no doubt this entire study was covered in prayer by you!

Julia and Cooper, I simply adore you. You kids have driven me to my knees many times, and for that I'm thankful. You are the reason I trust Jesus like I do, and you are the vessels through which He shows His love to me. Thank you for your patience and unconditional love for your mom (and for the hairdo's and foot massages when I needed them the most!)

Glenn, you were an answer to my prayer for a 'good' husband 20 years ago, and you still are! You made me believe I could do this. You appreciated my efforts, and you took care of everything else, so I could focus! Thank you for many coffee breaks and evening walks so I could use up my words. I love you for loving me!

My Jesus, You're my favorite of them all. I know You gave me this idea in the first place, so whether it was meant to bless five girls, or five hundred, I am at peace and overjoyed that You'd speak to me. Thank you for your personal love, always. My heart is Yours. This study is Yours. Use it as You will.

An inside perspective...

What do you do when you see your daughter struggling in her friendships? When everything in you wants to scream, "Not her! Don't be friends with her!", how do you exert your influence, while empowering her to make good choices on her own? How can you help her develop confidence in herself, create meaningful relationships, and invite God to sit on the throne of her heart ... without her realizing you're doing it?

What began as a desperate plea to God from a panicked mom, ended with a ten-week curriculum straight from heaven. I was prompted to read in Revelation - a book of the Bible I usually like to avoid, purely because it confuses me. My eyes were drawn to the verse that says, "I will also give that person a **white stone** with a new name written on it, known only to the one who receives it", Revelation 2:17(NIV). I knew in that moment that I wanted my daughter, Julia, to feel the joy that comes with knowing her heavenly Father has a special name just for her. That no matter what struggles she may face in life, she is loved personally, by the One who created her.

In this book you'll find ten lessons. I chose a small group of girls that Julia enjoyed spending time with, and whom I was comfortable having in our home every Thursday night, for ten weeks. You might use a different venue, and gather a larger crowd, depending on your desired outcome. This study is geared towards girls ages 8-12 years, and each week contains:

a. a theme with a key Bible verse
b. an activity or object lesson
c. a fill-in-the-blanks worksheet (Go to **tanyaschulz.com/ whitestone** for free printable worksheets.)
d. a chapter in the life of Zoey & Summer
e. discussion questions and Bible verses to look up (remember 'sword drills'?)
f. a challenge to complete before the next meeting

We had SO much fun with this! It's been 5 years since the original Whitestone Girls group was established, and we still talk about those special weeks together, and sit in awe of what God did in and through those young girls. One of the girls made a personal commitment to Jesus on week number eight! My hope is that you will see Him work in the ones you've chosen for your group, and that they, *and you* will experience His personal love!

This book, and anyone who puts it to use, has been covered in prayer! May it be used for His glory.

In this with you,

Tanya Schulz

Tanya's Ten Tips ...

1. **Pray.** Ask God who He wants in the group, when He wants you to start, and invite Him to lead it!

2. **Choose your timeline.** Will you meet every Wednesday for 10 weeks? Once a month for 10 months? After school? In the evenings?

3. **Invite the girls.** After speaking with the parents, put together a fun invitation for the girls with their names on it and leave it on their doorsteps! Perhaps individual white stones with the girl's name painted on it? Have fun with choosing something that will pique their interest and get them excited for something new!

4. **Prepare each lesson ahead of time.** Read through the material, print out the worksheets, create a comfy space, have a snack ready, prepare the supplies needed for any object lessons, turn some music on low, refill the toilet roll in the bathroom ... whatever you need to feel ready to receive the girls when they arrive.

5. **Keep the parents informed.** Send out an email to the parents, letting them know the schedule and what you'll be talking about. There's a tender balance of keeping conversations with the girls private and keeping parents in the loop and sharing special moments with them so they feel like they're part of the study. I loved being able

to report to a mom how patient her daughter was, or how creative another girl was. We moms love feedback about our kids - especially positive feedback!

6. **Greet the girls warmly and by name.** You never know what kind of day or week each girl has had. Making them feel welcome and wanted is a great way to soften their hearts, which in turn helps them feel ready to accept what God has planned for them during the study.

7. **Have a plan but be flexible.** I am a planner, and I was overly ready for each week we met. However, there were nights the girls were exceptionally squirrelly, having trouble focusing, or couldn't stop giggling. I had to remind myself what my mission was - to create a bond between these girls with the common denominator being Jesus. If we needed to stop, and run around the block before diving in again, we did it. If you have prayed ahead of time, you can trust God is at work, even if it feels chaotic at times.

8. **Allow room for questions and be ready to be stumped!** You may see a discussion going a certain way, and then it doesn't. Just know that if they're asking questions at all, it means you've created an environment that is safe to do so. Go with it (unless it's completely off topic). If you don't know the answer, or want to give a thoughtful answer, it's okay to take your time. Tell them you'll get back to them - then do it. You might address the question as a group or send a special note to one girl.

9. **Have some consistency, AND some surprises.** You're bound to have a variety of personalities in your group. Some girls will find comfort in the familiar (starting every meeting by asking them to tell you their memory verse), and others will live for the unknown (What kind of snack will there be tonight?).

10. **Remember it's not all up to you.** You are doing a great thing for these girls. You're loving them in a consistent, practical, fun, and memorable way. You may have girls ask you insightful questions about Jesus, and it'll make your soul soar! Or you may think they're getting nothing out of it all. Trust the Holy Spirit to do the growing. You just plant the seeds.

A Template for Your Time...

Warm Up (15 min)

Greet the girls.
Award stickers for each box they complete on their chart (see the sample chart of specific goals for each week).
Ask them a key question (What were the highs and lows of your week? What was the highlight of your day so far?) and encourage the girls to listen to each other's answer.
Have a simple finger snack available to keep their mouths busy while listening.

Activity/ Story/ Discussion (40 min)

Complete the prepared activity (you may need to move to another room). Any supplies you'll need will be listed at the bottom of your lesson layout. The story and discussion may be part of the activity OR you may need to complete the activity, then move somewhere the girls can do their fill-in-the-blanks worksheets at a table and enjoy a snack while answering the discussion questions.

Sword Drill (15 min)

Introduce the books of the Bible to the girls. You can teach them a song, using a YouTube video, or find another way to teach it to them. Review it every week!

Show them how to look up scriptures with just a Bible reference and explain that it will take time at first. Have a competition to see who can find the scripture fastest. Whoever gets it first, can help a friend find it too.

NOTE: _We had girls who knew the Books of the Bible already, and girls who had never opened a Bible before. By the end of the ten weeks, I had to hide some of the Bibles to level the playing field! They all LOVED this old-school competition._

Prayer Time (15 min)

Make time to go around the room and have the girls share their prayer requests and praise reports.

We used the T.A.P. method when we prayed - **T**hank God for who He is and what He's already done, **A**sk Him for what's on your heart, and **P**raise Him in advance for what He's going to do! Consider keeping a journal for these prayers.

Wrap Up (5 min)

Have them write the key verse on their worksheets, so they can learn it for the next week.

Present the challenge for the week!

Table of Contents

We are...

My Whitestone Girl Chart

	W 01/22	H 01/29	I 02/05	T 02/12	E 02/19	S 02/26	T 03/05	O 03/12	N 03/19	E 03/26
I'm here! (and I remember one thing)										
I know my verse :)										
I met the challenge!										
I brought my Bible!										

20 stickers = small prize   30 stickers = medium prize   40 stickers = very special prize!!!

The Books of the Bible ...

(use colored highlighters & highlight chunks of books to make it easier to memorize!)

Old Testament

Genesis
Exodus
Leviticus
Numbers
Deuteronomy
Joshua
Judges
Ruth
1 Samuel
2 Samuel
1 Kings
2 Kings
1 Chronicles
2 Chronicles
Ezra
Nehemiah
Esther
Job
Psalms
Proverbs

Ecclesiastes
Song of Solomon
Isaiah
Jeremiah
Lamentations
Ezekiel
Daniel
Hosea
Joel
Amos
Obadiah
Jonah
Micah
Nahum
Habakkuk
Zephaniah
Haggai
Zechariah
Malachi

New Testament

Matthew
Mark
Luke
John
Acts
Romans
1 Corinthians
2 Corinthians
Galatians
Ephesians
Philippians
Colossians
1 Thessalonians
2 Thessalonians

1 Timothy
2 Timothy
Titus
Philemon
Hebrews
James
1 Peter
2 Peter
1 John
2 John
3 John
Jude
Revelation

lesson one

Women in the Making ...
Girls for Now

Women in the Making ... Girls for Now

Week 1 Layout

Trust in the Lord with all your heart and lean not
on your own understanding; in all your ways submit
to him, and he will make your paths straight.
Proverbs 3:5–6 (NIV)

Warm Up

Welcome the girls and have them begin designing their own binder covers. While they work, ask them to say their names, grades, favorite colors, and the activity/sport they enjoy most.

Activity/Story/Discussion

Have the girls design their own binder covers with stickers and colors that are fitting for them right now. Insert the Whitestone girl's chart, table of contents, and books of the Bible list in each binder ahead of time.

Overview

Share your excitement about having the girls meet each week and the hope that they'll grow in their friendships and learn stuff that they'll take back to their schools and activities. Point out the table of contents and the plan for each week– hear a story, talk about it, do something special together, learn to find verses in the Bible, hide God's Word in their hearts, and leave with a challenge!

Main Idea

Trust God with your *future* and be *thankful* for today.

Fill in the blanks together

Go to **tanyaschulz.com/whitestone** for free printable worksheets.

Story/Discussion

Introduction to Zoey and Summer–To Change or Not to Change

Sword Drill

Listen to a books of the Bible song then look up the following scriptures together.
Romans 14:6
1 Thessalonians 5:18
Psalm 37:5
Romans 15:13
Proverbs 3:5

Discussion Questions

1. What's great about being the age you are right now?
2. What's the harm in wanting to grow up fast? Or act older than you really are?

3. What do we need to do to make sure our lives stay on a straight path?
4. Who in your life has modeled a straight path?
5. How can we show God we trust Him and show thanks for today?

Prayer Time

Introduce the TAP (thanks, ask, praise) idea and ask for any prayer requests.

Wrap Up

Make it Real

This week, when you see a teenaged girl texting or talking on her phone, bust into a silly dance—because you can!

Hide It in Your Heart

Have the girls rewrite the verse in their own handwriting to help them memorize it!

Supplies needed:

binders with a clear front pocket
paper
markers/crayons
stickers
snacks
pens to fill in the blanks
a Bible for each girl (encourage them to bring their own)
3 Printouts: Table of contents, Books of the Bible, your own chart creation

---

Women in the Making ... Girls for Now

Trust in the Lord with all your heart and lean not
on your own understanding; in all your ways submit
to him, and he will make your paths straight.
Proverbs 3:5–6 (NIV)

Main Idea

Trust God with your _____
and be _____ for today.

Think About It

1. What's great about being the age you are?
2. What's the harm in wanting to grow up fast? Or act older than you really are?
3. What do we need to do as Christ followers to make sure our lives stay on a straight path?
4. Who in your life has modeled a straight path?
5. How can we show God we trust Him and show thanks for today?

Make It Real!

This week when you see a teenaged girl texting or talking on her phone, bust into a silly dance–just because you can!

Hidin' it in my heart ...

Introducing Zoey and Summer

I'd like to introduce you to two girls who have been friends for, well, pretty much forever. Zoey is the energetic, creative, and whimsical one, and Summer is the organized, even keeled, and rational type of girl. Together they make a pretty cool team. They share secrets, laugh at each other's jokes and blunders, and come up with some amazing skits and fashion shows to put on for whoever will watch! The girls love spending time together, but every once in a while, they need time apart because, as their moms put it, they get into "sister mode." I'm pretty sure that's code for "they're fighting too much."

Zoey just celebrated her birthday, and among the gifts of clothes, hair accessories, and cash from relatives, her favorite gift was a new iPhone. All the girls oohed and aahed over this cool handheld device and imagined the fun Zoey would have playing games, listening to music, and texting friends. Summer couldn't help but feel a little envious.

But it wasn't until a few weeks later that Summer would realize this gift would have a huge impact on her friendship with Zoey. All of a sudden, Zoey wasn't into creating skits or finding new styles for fashion shows. All she wanted to do was play with her now iPhone. When Summer mentioned this to Zoey, she apologized and made more of an effort to play with Summer, but it seemed like every five minutes she would glance at her iPhone to see if she'd received any new texts. Summer was really discouraged and confused. She wanted to be happy for Zoey, but she missed the old Zoey who would be silly with her and wasn't so attached to technology. She started to wonder if playing with barbies and dressing up was for little girls, and Zoey had moved up to the big league where technology was the new cool thing. Summer wondered if Zoey had grown up, and that if she still wanted to be friends with Zoey, would she have to hurry and grow up too? She didn't know what to think or what to do.

Discussion Questions

1. Have you ever experienced something like this?
2. Do you feel pressure to grow up quickly or give up some things you used to love in order to feel "cool"?
3. Is it true that iPhones are more grown up than putting on fashion shows? Or can you enjoy both?
4. Is it wrong to like the new technology we have these days?
5. What do you think Summer should do?
6. What do you think Zoey should do?

lesson two

Here on Purpose

Here on Purpose

Week 2 Layout

Before I formed you in the womb I knew you,
before you were born I set you apart.
Jeremiah 1:5 (NIV)

Warm Up

Welcome the girls, offer a snack, and ask about their weeks. Sticker their charts as earned. Bring them into the kitchen after everyone has had a chance to share.

Activity/Story/Discussion

Set up stations or mini barricades between the girls so they can't see one another's canvases. Give each girl her own set of paints to paint: a sun, grass, some flowers, a bird in the sky, a little fort or house. They can paint the items wherever they want and with whatever colors they choose.

Overview

Point out that each girl has her own gifts and talents and personality and that each girl has her own school, activities outside of school, and neighborhood. Explain that even though these girls may hear the same teachings in church or during Whitestone Girls meetings and maybe even from their parents—just like they all got the same instructions for painting—the results will look different. God doesn't want robots. He designed you in a special way to do special things in the special place He put you.

Story/Discussion

Zoey and Summer's Special Assignments!

Main Idea

We are all *made* differently and *placed* differently for a reason. Ask yourself, "How will God *use me* where I am?"

Fill in the blanks together

Go to **tanyaschulz.com/whitestone** for free printable worksheets.

Sword Drill

Listen to books of the Bible song then look up these scriptures together.
Psalm 139:14
Galatians 1:15
Esther 4:11-14
Jeremiah 1:5

Discuss

1. Tell us what makes you unique.
2. Describe the family and school/activities you are part of.

3. Can you think of a reason God might've put you in this family? In this school situation? In your neighborhood?
4. How do you know if you're fulfilling God's purpose for you in these places?
5. Who in your life can you start praying for today?

Prayer Time

Do the TAP (thanks, ask, praise) idea and pray for the person they choose for the week.

Wrap Up

Make it Real

Think of one person in your life who you'll pray for this week then find a way to encourage that person in your own unique way!

Hide It in Your Heart

Have the girls rewrite the verse in their own handwriting to help them memorize it!

Supplies needed:

canvases
paints
paint brushes
small cups of water
paper towels
snacks
pens to fill in the blanks
a Bible for each girl

Here on Purpose

Before I formed you in the womb I knew you,
before you were born I set you apart.
Jeremiah 1:5(NIV)

Main Idea

We are all _____ differently
and _____ differently
for a reason. Ask yourself, "How will God
_____ _____ where I am?"

Think About It

1. Tell us what makes you unique.
2. Describe the family and school/activities you are part of.
3. Can you think of a reason God might've put you in this family? In this school situation? In your neighborhood?
4. How do you know if you're fulfilling God's purpose for you in these places?
5. Who in your life can you start praying for today?

Make It Real!

Think of one person in your life who you'll pray for this week then find a way to encourage that person in your own unique way!

Hidin' it in my heart ...

Zoey and Summer's Special Assignments!

Zoey and Summer used to be in the same class at school, but for some reasons only her parents knew, Summer became a homeschool student this year. Both of the girls were unhappy about this decision. Zoey had lots of friends at school, but no one understood her like Summer. Who would she play with at recess now? And why did she feel like no one really wanted her around? It was hard for Zoey to be her peppy self, when inside she felt self-conscious and unsure of herself without her closest friend close by.

Summer was upset too. She loves her mom and all, but she wasn't super keen on being with her *all* day *every* day. What about her friends? Would they forget about her? And how is she supposed to be a "light" in her school if everyone around her already knows Jesus?

The girls were swinging together in Summer's backyard, sharing their frustrations. Zoey dragged her toe until she stopped swinging and said,

"I think we should pray about this. Maybe God will let us go back to the way things were." So, they prayed. They asked God to make their situation better ... to fix it so they could be themselves again.

A few days later Summer was sitting by the window in her living room, trying to do her math work, when she noticed her old neighbor from across the street start walking toward her mailbox. At the same time, Summer saw a teenaged girl walking her chihuahua straight toward that same mailbox, and texting at the same time. The collision happened before Summer could get to the door to warn her neighbor. The elderly lady tripped over the little dog and landed right on her knee! The teenaged girl apologized and then scurried away, her yappy dog in tow. Summer yelled to her mom for help, then rushed to her neighbor to help her up, but she was in too much pain to stand. Summer's mom called for an ambulance to take the poor woman to the hospital, and they later found out her knee was broken!

A few days after the dog-tripping incident, Summer's neighbor was brought back home. Summer watched her awkwardly make her way on crutches from the car to her front door. She felt bad for the lady. How would she take care of herself? Maybe there was something Summer could do to be helpful. She asked her mom about this and they came up with a plan and put it on paper. Within 20 minutes, Summer was skipping across the street, excited about her idea. She knocked on the door and waited for what seemed like a long time for the woman to answer. When the door finally opened, Summer said, "Hi! I'm Summer from across the street. I'm homeschooled now and have a pretty flexible schedule. I was wondering if I could help you with a few things while your knee is healing?" She handed the piece of paper to the woman, and as the woman read all the items on the list that Summer wanted to help with – taking out the trash, vacuuming the house, collecting her mail, and feeding the cat – tears welled up in her eyes. She smiled at Summer and said, "You are such an angel! My kids live far away, and I have no one to help me. I was *just* praying to God for help … and here you are!"

Meanwhile, at Zoey's school, another adventure had begun. A new girl joined the class and it appeared she would not fit in very well. She had two long pig-tails – one dark black and the other a bright pink! She wore brightly colored clothes and lots of accessories that jingled and jangled when she walked. She was friendly enough, but her appearance made the girls in the class want to stay away from her, and Zoey noticed the girl's confidence start to wane as the days went by.

Zoey kind of admired the girl for being so bold in the way she dressed. Perhaps this girl was a whimsical girl just like Zoey! She remembered a lesson she learned in church awhile back, about loving the unlovable. She took a deep breath, walked up to the new girl and said, "Hey! I'm Zoey. Wanna have lunch with me today?" The girl was both surprised and delighted at the invitation. She accepted gratefully and after a full week of lunches together Zoey found that this girl was really nice. She'd had a bad experience being bullied in her old school and that's why she got transferred to this new school. Zoey was able to introduce her to more of the girls, and eventually she became one of the crowd instead of the girl standing outside of the crowd.

Zoey and Summer couldn't wait to get together to talk about what had happened in the past couple of weeks. Their moms let them walk to their special meeting spot. They sat down on the curb and shared their news with each other. After about fifteen minutes, Summer finally said, "Remember how we prayed for God to help us? So that we could be ourselves again? I think He had something better in mind, don't you?"

lesson three

In it to Win it

In it to Win it

Week 3- Layout

Love the Lord your God with all your heart and with
all your soul and with all your mind and with all your
strength ... Love your neighbor as yourself.
Mark 12:30–31 (NIV)

Warm Up

Welcome the girls in and award them their stickers as earned.

Main Idea

Our goal is *heaven*. How do we *get there*? (hint:
Romans 10:9) Ask yourself, "What *treasures*
am I storing up along the way?"

Fill in the blanks of our main idea and go over the next verse.

Go to **tanyaschulz.com/whitestone** for free printable
worksheets.

Activity/Story/Discussion

Lead the girls on a scenario scavenger hunt with printed scenarios pre-planted on telephone poles, fence posts, and stop signs along a specific route (see the scenario page). Walk around the neighborhood, stopping to read scenarios and answering what they would do in each case. Ask them how they could be storing up treasures in heaven in each scenario. Allow discussion and silliness between the girls along the way

Table Time:
Have the table set with name cards and special treats for each girl

Discuss

1. Are you going to heaven? How do you know?
2. What do you think about most often? What is your heart set on?
3. What's the difference between treasures on earth and treasures in heaven (list)?
4. How can we store up treasures in heaven?

Sword drill

Listen to books of the Bible song then look up these scriptures together.
Romans 10:9
Acts 20:24
Hebrews 12:1
Luke 12:32-34
Matthew 6:3–4, 20
Mark 12:30–31

Prayer Time

Pray together about their assignment and how to be mindful of storing up treasures in heaven. Give them the opportunity to accept Christ.

Wrap Up

Make it Real

Sneaky Servant Mission (Matt 6:3–4) Serve someone this week without getting caught! Some examples include taking out the trash, cleaning a bathroom, picking up litter, or folding the laundry.

Hide It In Your Heart

Have the girls write out their verses in their own handwriting.

Supplies needed:

cut out the scenarios provided and tape them around the neighborhood (on stop signs, mailboxes, etc) ahead of time
name cards for each girl
special treats
pens for fill in the blanks
a Bible for each girl

𝓘n it to win it

Love the Lord your God with all your HEART and with
all your SOUL and with all your MIND and with all your
STRENGTH ... Love your neighbor as yourself ...
Mark 12:30–31 (NIV)

Main Idea

Our goal is _____. How do we
_____? (hint: Romans 10:9)
Ask yourself, "What _____
am I storing up along the way?"

Think About It?

1. Are you going to heaven? How do you know?
2. What do you think about most often? What is your heart set on?
3. What's the difference between treasures in heaven and treasures on earth?
4. How can you store up treasures in heaven, while you're here on earth?

Treasures on Earth　　　　　Treasures in Heaven

Make it Real!

Sneaky Servant Mission (shhhh!). Serve someone this week without getting caught! Some examples include taking out the trash, cleaning a bathroom, picking up litter, or folding the laundry. Remember Matthew 6:3–4!

Hidin' it in my heart ...

Scenario Scavenger Hunt

Ask "How can I store up treasures in heaven" in each situation?

1. You're in class and a student is called on to answer a simple question. She answers it totally wrong and your classmates start to snicker and whisper, "Is she stupid?" The girl hears them and shrinks back in silence. What do you do?

    a. *laugh quietly with the group*
    b. *say "duh!" with a funny face that makes everyone laugh*
    c. *not join in the snickering and change the subject*
    d. *change the subject, then go up to her privately and tell her about a time YOU felt embarrassed*

2. You're playing soccer and make a beautiful goal, but the referee says it doesn't count because you touched the ball with your hand before scoring. You *know* you didn't do a hand ball. What do you do?

    a. *tell the ref he made a mistake*
    b. *kick the ball super hard and go tell all your friends the ref is horrible*
    c. *shrug it off and try to get another goal!*

3. You're celebrating your birthday and get some awesome gifts from your friends. Unfortunately, you didn't get the *one* thing you really wanted. Two days later you get fifty dollars in the mail from a relative. This is exactly the amount you need to buy that special item. You go to church with the money in your pocket because you plan to go shopping afterwards. While in church, you learn about a family whose house just burned down in a fire. The teacher encourages you to help in any way you can. Do you:

    a. *give the fifty dollars to the family, knowing they need it more than you need your special item?*

b. *give twenty-five dollars to the family and put off buying your special item until you can earn more money?*
c. *keep the money in your pocket and don't say anything?*
d. *keep the money in your pocket and try to think of another way to help the family?*

4. A girl in your school hears you talking about church. She tells you she doesn't have a Bible and her family doesn't have enough money to buy one. Do you:

a. *say, "that's too bad. Maybe you can ask for one for your birthday?"*
b. *tell her she doesn't really need one because no one reads them anyways?*
c. *talk to your parents about giving her yours, or buying her one of her own as a gift?*

5. You're in church and are surrounded by Whitestone girls except for one other girl. She feels left out because she's the only one not in the group. Do you:

a. *tell her it's a great group, but she can't be part of it because she wasn't invited?*
b. *talk about everything you do at Whitestone girls, hoping she'll think it's cool and really wish she could be in it?*
c. *go out of your way to be friendly to the girl and sacrifice time with your Whitestone friends. You'll see them this week anyways!*
d. *put into practice all the stuff you're learning at Whitestone girls (like showing love to those around you when you're given the opportunity ... "here for a purpose") without talking about the girl's club. Hopefully the other girls will see what you're doing and back you up with more love for the girl!!!*

6. Your teacher announces that you're having a spelling test and you haven't studied! The girl sitting beside you is a

great speller, so you sneak a peek at her page when you're not sure how to spell a word. The teacher doesn't catch you and you end up getting 100%! Do you:

a. *give a sigh of relief that you didn't get caught and tell yourself not to cheat again!*
b. *admit to the teacher that you cheated and apologize, knowing there will be consequences?*
c. *tell only your closest friend what you did, and make her promise not to tell?*

7. You have a hang-out date set up with a new friend at school and are really excited about it! The girl lives close by, so the plan is to walk to your house after school on Friday. The bell rings and you start your walk, but half-way there you see a dog wandering the streets, with no owner around. The dog looks scared and unsure where to go. Do you:

a. *keep on walking, hoping the dog will be okay?*
b. *try to call the dog to check for an address on his collar, then tell your parents later?*
c. *knock on some doors in the neighborhood trying to find the owner, even though you know it'll make you late to your hang-out?*

8. Your little brother has a soccer game and you have to go too because there's no one else who can stay home with you. You're not happy about going to the game, especially because there's a little girl there that always follows you around. She drives you crazy. You show up at the game and sure enough, she's there. Do you:

a. *pull out a book and start reading, hoping she won't bother you?*
b. *avoid making eye contact with her and pretend to be interested in your brother's game JUST so you don't have to play with her?*

c. *decide it's just one hour of your time, and take the time to talk and play with her?*

9. You find a dollar bill on the ground when walking through a parking lot with your dad. There's a dollar store close by and your dad gives you permission to buy some candy with your dollar. Just outside of the store, there's a homeless man begging for money or food. Do you:

   a. *smile at him and walk by, excited about the candy you'll buy?*
   b. *feel a little guilty about the fact that he has nothing, but decide it's his own fault and keep on walking?*
   c. *buy your candy, then share some with him as you leave the store?*
   d. *decide that maybe you found the dollar so you could share it with this man. You can live without candy!*

10. Your assignment this week is to go on a sneaky servant mission! You ask your parents if you can borrow their rake and go next door to rake up your neighbor's leaves, since he's an elderly man and it's really hard for him to get around. They give you permission and even offer to help. You clean the yard up beautifully and feel really good about helping out, but you are disappointed to find out your neighbor gave the credit to another kid on the street. Do you:

    a. *make sure he knows it was YOU who cleaned up his yard?*
    b. *tell the other kid on your street that the man thought it was him who cleaned the yard, but really it was you? Then hope the kid will tell your neighbor.*
    c. *complain to your parents that it's not fair that you did the work, and nobody knows it?*
    d. *say nothing, knowing that your heavenly Father saw your good deed and will reward you in secret.*

11. You're trying hard to get closer to God, but you don't understand everything you read in your Bible. You know it's a good thing to fill your mind with God's truth and that some of your friends listen to Christian music for that reason. Your friends at school are talking about the newest artist and how great her music is. Do you:

    a. *ask your parents if you can get the latest music release so you can fit in with your friends at school?*
    b. *ask your parents if you can buy some new Christian music so you can fill your mind with things that honor Christ?*
    c. *listen to Christian music with your Christian friends but listen to worldly music with your school friends?*
    d. *introduce your school friends to some cool new Christian music?*

12. You've finished all your homework and it's only Wednesday! You've had time to play outside and watch a movie on TV and now your mom says you need to have some quiet time in your room before bed. You have the choice of playing with your toys, reading a book, or cleaning your room. You think about our lesson on storing up treasures in heaven and decide to:

    a. *clean your room as a surprise to your parents. They'd never expect it and you know it will make them happy.*
    b. *play with your toys. After all, you've earned it!*
    c. *do a quick tidy of your room so you can at least see the floor, then curl up on your bed with your journal and Bible. You want to know more about what God has planned for you and can't wait to spend time with Him!*

lesson four

Truly Beautiful ... and Fruity

Truly Beautiful and Fruity

Week 4- Layout

Remain in me, as I also remain in you. No branch can
bear fruit by itself; it must remain in the vine. Neither
can you bear fruit unless you remain in me.
John 15:4 (NIV)

Warm Up

Welcome the girls and give them stickers in their charts as
earned. Go outside to look at a leafy plant or tree that has
roots that go deep down into the moist ground. Compare the
green leaves on that tree to a branch that is *not* attached to the
tree—one that is dry and lifeless—and explain the importance
of the roots, and how they draw water to the branch and the
leaves.

Activity/Story/Discussion

Main Idea

True beauty starts from the *inside* (1 Peter 3:3–4), and
can be seen in the *fruit* you produce (Galatians 5:22).

Fill in the blanks and look up the verses that support the idea.

Go to **tanyaschulz.com/whitestone** for free printable worksheets.

Activity (Play dough art)

Move into a room with space for each girl around a table. Each girl should have a spot with a piece of white paper, a brown and green crayon, multiple colors of play dough, and small clips of paper with the fruits of the Spirit written on them. (go to **tanyaschulz.com**/whitestone for a free printable worksheet) Have them draw a tree trunk with long roots, and a green tree-top on the white paper. After this, the girls will create fruit shapes out of the play dough and place them on the tree with the paper clips/labels on each fruit, so they can visualize the different fruits of the Spirit.

Story

Zoey and Summer - Deep Roots Means Juicy Fruits

Sword Drill

Listen to books of the Bible song then look up these scriptures together.
Proverbs 31:30
Jeremiah 17:8
Matthew 7:16–20
1 Peter 3:3–4
John 15:4, 16

Prayer Time

Each girl shares a prayer request and the requests are divided among the girls to be prayed over together.

Wrap Up

Make it Real

Read your Bible every day this week. It can be a page, a story, a chapter, or a stretch of 10 minutes before bed. Ask Jesus to help you to understand what you read before you start, and just see what you learn!

Hide it in Your Heart

Have the girls write out their memory verses for the week.

Supplies needed:

white paper
brown and green crayons
play dough of multiple colors
fruit labels cut from the worksheet
snacks
pens for fill in the blanks
a Bible for each girl

Truly beautiful ... and fruity

Remain in me, as I also remain in you. No branch can
bear fruit by itself; it must remain in the vine. Neither
can you bear fruit unless you remain in me.
John 15:4 (NIV)

Main Idea

True beauty starts from the
_____ (1 Peter 3:3—4)
and can be seen in the _____
you produce (Gal 5:22).

Think About It?

1. Do you see yourself as beautiful? Why or why not?
2. Which fruit of the Spirit do you see displayed in your life?
3. Which fruit of the Spirit do you hope will grow?
4. How often do you talk to Jesus? Read your Bible? Listen to music that honors Him?
5. What can you do differently this week to build stronger roots and add to your fruity beauty?

Make it Real!

Read your Bible every day this week. It can be a page, a story, a chapter, or a stretch of 10 minutes before bed. Ask Jesus to help you understand what you read before you start and see what you learn!

Sun

Mon

Tues

Wed

Thurs

Fri

Hidin' it in my heart ...

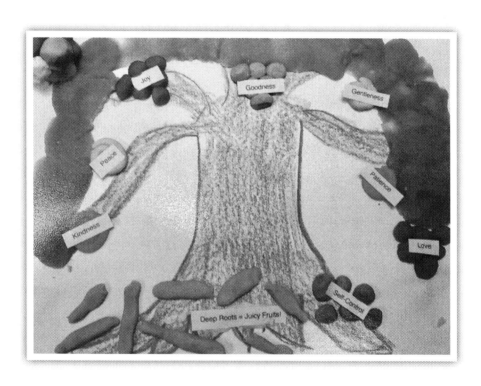

Zoey and Summer - Deep Roots means Juicy Fruits!

Zoey and Summer were excited about how God was using them in their different situations —Zoey at her school, and Summer in her neighborhood. It inspired them to start reading their Bibles more and begin each day by saying, "Thank you Jesus for this day. I can't *wait* to see what you have planned today!" The girls even came up with a special plan to meet at the curb every Wednesday after school to talk about what they'd read in the Bible, and to challenge each other to practice what they'd read. They were getting rooted in God! What they didn't realize, was that their roots were about to be tested.

The rain just wouldn't let up. The weatherman said the rainfall this winter was more than the city had seen for 30 years, and it wasn't going to stop any time soon. Summer's parents were concerned because they lived in a valley where the rainwater collected and didn't have anywhere to drain out. They tried to divert the water away from the house, but it was no use. When Summer's family got home from church one Sunday morning, their house was flooded! There was so much water damage, they couldn't stay there. Staying in a hotel would be too expensive. Their only option was to live with Summer's mom's sister - cranky Aunt Shirley. Her house was cluttered and smelled like brussels sprouts. Aunt Shirley did *not* have Jesus in her life, and it showed. She wasn't a happy person and every conversation was about what this person did wrong, or why that person is no good. Honestly, it was depressing being stuck in this house. Summer stopped reading her Bible and woke up dreading the days instead of being excited about starting each day with Jesus. By the time Wednesday rolled around, Summer was as negative and cranky as her cranky Aunt Shirley!

During the time Summer was kicked out of her house, Zoey had developed a problem of her own. She woke up one day, said good morning to Jesus, and hopped out of bed. When she passed by her bedroom mirror, she stopped in horror. What were all those red bumps on her face? She rushed to the bathroom and scrubbed her face, hoping the bumps would go away, but nope. She was standing there with tears in her eyes when her mom found her. "Oh, sweet pea!" her mom said in that comforting voice, which only added to Zoey's tears. She explained to Zoey that the bumps were pimples and just a natural part of growing up. She assured her that they would go away in time and that Zoey should just wash her face daily and try not to touch it. Zoey didn't know how she was going to go to school like this. Everyone would laugh, or worse, look at her and talk behind her back. She thought she'd be sick. She got dressed and went to her cozy corner in her room, pulled out her Bible and opened it up to 1 Peter 3:3–4 (NIV). She read the verse that said, "Your beauty should not come from outward adornment, such as braided hair and the wearing of gold jewelry and fine clothes. Instead it should be that of your *inner self,* the unfading beauty of a gentle and quiet spirit, which is of great worth in God's sight." Immediately Zoey lifted her eyes to heaven and said, "Jesus, I'm scared to go to school with my face like this. But you said that my beauty comes from inside ... from a quiet and gentle spirit. And I trust you. Please help me be beautiful from the inside out today." She went to school with the usual spring in her step and smile on her face. And to her delight, no one mentioned anything about her face. In fact, one girl even said she looked radiant that day!

The clouds broke open Wednesday morning, so the girls were able to meet at the curb as usual. Summer was there first, slumped over and looking at the ground. Zoey skipped up to her with a cheery hello but was met with a less than friendly look. "How's your week going, Summer?" Zoey asked. "Are you making the most of your time at your Aunt Shirley's?" Summer looked grimly at Zoey and said, "I wish I could be as cheery as you, Zoey, but I feel grumpy and mad and sometimes I just want to cry!" Zoey sat down beside her and put her arm around her friend. "I'm so sorry you're having a rough time. Let's pray that God will refuel your joy and help you show love to your Aunt Shirley. It sounds like she needs a bite of your juicy fruit!" They laughed together, knowing Zoey was talking about the fruits of the Spirit – love, joy, peace, patience, kindness, goodness, gentleness and self-control – not real fruit!

"You know what?" Summer started. "I haven't been talking to God much OR reading my Bible. I'm afraid my fruit isn't very juicy right now. Maybe you can pray for my roots to go deeper first. Then the fruit will come naturally." So, they did just that.

Discussion Questions

1. Who was more beautiful in this story – Zoey or Summer? Why?
2. How did Zoey and Summer react differently to their hard circumstances?
3. If you're reading the Bible and praying, does it mean you'll never get upset?
4. How does staying connected to God (having strong roots) help you produce juicy fruits like love, joy, peace, patience, kindness, goodness, gentleness and self-control?

Deep Roots = Juicy Fruits!
Love
Joy
Peace
Patience
Kindness
Goodness
Gentleness
Self-Control

Deep Roots = Juicy Fruits!
Love
Joy
Peace
Patience
Kindness
Goodness
Gentleness
Self-Control

Deep Roots = Juicy Fruits!
Love
Joy
Peace
Patience
Kindness
Goodness
Gentleness
Self-Control

Deep Roots = Juicy Fruits!
Love
Joy
Peace
Patience
Kindness
Goodness
Gentleness
Self-Control

lesson five

Eating Flour ... Picturing Cake

Eating Flour Picturing Cake

Week 5- Layout

And we know that in all things God works for
the good of those who love him, who have
been called according to his purpose.
Romans 8:28 (NIV)

Warm Up

Welcome the girls and give them stickers in their charts as
earned.

Activity/Story/Discussion

Go to the kitchen to bake cupcakes together. Have the girls
taste-test the individual ingredients and explain that although
some of the ingredients taste yucky, (much like some things
in life are awful), they all mix together to create a yummy
cake (like how God takes all the hurts and bad stuff to make
something good). Put the cupcakes in the oven to bake, then
head into your meeting space.

Main Idea

There will be *trouble* in this world (John 16:33), but God uses it all to make something *good!* When you go through a hard time, remember it's just one *ingredient* needed to make something yummy!

Fill in the blanks and look up the verses that support the idea.

Go to **tanyaschulz.com/whitestone** for free printable worksheets.

Story

Read out loud the different stories provided by the girls' moms, that tell about a time they went through something "bad", but it turned out "good". Have the girls guess which mom wrote each one (Samples provided).

Sword Drill

Play the books of the Bible song, then look up the scriptures below. Make it more challenging for the girls who are consistently the fastest, by hiding their Bibles ahead of time.
John 16:33
James 1:2–4
Proverbs 3:5
Psalm 145:8–9
Romans 8:28

Ask "Think about it" questions while the girls frost & decorate their cupcakes

1. When you invite Jesus into your heart, do all your troubles fade away?

2. Do good things happen to good people, and bad things to bad people?
3. Tell us about a time you were sad about something, but it all turned out okay. What happened?
4. What's a good thing that comes out of going through trials? (James 1:2–4)
5. Why did we bake a cake tonight?

Prayer Time

Each girl is invited to share a request, and then the requests are divided among the girls to be prayed over together.

Wrap Up

Make it Real

Come back next time and tell us about a time this week, when you were unhappy about something, but remembered (or saw) it was all part of the plan for something good!

Hide It in Your Heart

Have the girls write out their memory verse for the week.

Supplies needed:

ingredients for cupcakes, in individual bowls
oven for baking
stories from the girls' moms (collect ahead of time)
snacks
pens for fill in the blanks
a Bible for each girl

Eating Flour ... Picturing Cake

And we know that in all things God works for
the good of those who love him, who have
been called according to his purpose.
Romans 8:28 (NIV)

Main Idea

There will be _____ in this
world (John 16:33), but God uses it all to
make something _____! When
you go through a hard time, remember
it's just one _____
needed to make something yummy!

Think About It?

1. When you invite Jesus into your heart, do all your troubles
   fade away?
2. Do good things happen to good people, and bad things to
   bad people?
3. Tell us about a time you were sad about something, but it
   all turned out okay. What happened?
4. What's a good thing that comes out of going through trials?
   (James 1:2–4)
5. Why did we bake a cake tonight?

Make it Real!

Come back next time and tell us about a time this week when you were unhappy about something, but remembered it was all part of the plan for something good!

Hidin' it in my heart ...

Sample Whitestone "Mom Stories"

... in response to the question,
"Tell about a time in your life when something
bad turned into something good."

When I was nine, my much older sister decided to get married. I did everything with my sister. and she took me everywhere and did a lot of really cool things with me. She was the one who took me to get my ears pierced. She taught me how to do my make-up and trained me on the fundamentals of good shopping. I thought that surely this was all coming to an end with her moving out and getting married.

The big day came and went, and I cried like a big baby the whole time. I cried because I had no one to share my room with any longer. I cried because home seemed to me to be a boring place without her at home. I cried because she wouldn't be there every day like I had always known.

Soon after she got married, I noticed that she came around home a lot. Her new husband was taking some night classes and she enjoyed coming home and even *chose* to come home to be with me. It occurred to me that even though she wasn't living with us any longer, I was getting something special here. I was getting the better part of my sister (the part that didn't fight with me) and that I was enjoying many more good memories and milestones with her.

My story doesn't end there. God taught me that through this, I was also getting another really cool big brother who would also take me places and do fun stuff with me. Three years later, he would be the one to baptize me, which was a very precious experience. Another bonus was that a couple of years later, I finally got the little sister I always wanted when my niece was born. God certainly turned what I thought was a bad change into something beautiful in my life!

Julie.

When I turned 16 my parents bought me a car. It was really old, and really ugly. The total opposite of cool. It was *huge*! It belonged to an elderly man who never drove it ... and I hated it (I was a brat!).

Well, that same car saved me from getting really hurt in an accident. I got hit from behind while I was stopped at a light, and the guy totaled my car, but I barely felt it because the car was a huge safe tank!

Angie

I switched schools in 4th grade because my older brother needed a fresh start ... away from some trouble-making friends. He had to change schools, so I had to change schools. I was super sad about this because I had a good group of friends AND the school I was going to was close enough to my house that I could walk home for lunch every day. The new school would be too far to do this.

The first day of fourth grade was awful. My teacher was mean, I didn't know anyone, and they told us to put our names on the right side of our papers. That may not seem like a big deal, but I had *always* put my name on the left side of the paper, and this little change put me over the edge. I got sick to my stomach and had to go home! I missed the first 2 days of school and was scared to death to go back. As far as I was concerned, this was the worst school ever and I would be sad every day I had to go there. But guess what happened? I discovered a huge rock on one side of the school field. I started taking my Bible there at lunch time and would read it to whomever wanted to come with me. I began a Bible study called, the "Christian Rock" and only girls were allowed. I brought all the Bibles I could find in our house and shared them with my friends. We did sword drills, sang songs that I'd learned in Sunday School and just talked about Jesus. Every lunch time I would ask the girls if they wanted to invite Jesus into their hearts and a few did!

I was looking up friends on Facebook a few years ago and learned that one of the girls — her name was Cathy Tilbury — is still a Christian today and loves Jesus! I only went to that school for two years before we moved away, and although I still have some bad memories from that school, I'm thankful that I was able to share my faith and lead my very first Bible study ... at 9 years old!

Tanya

When I was in first grade my teachers told my parents that they wanted me to re-do first grade because my reading wasn't as good as all the rest of the kids in the class. As I got older, I realized that I wasn't like the other kids. They were all amazing readers and spellers, and I struggled so much with reading and spelling. There was a huge part of me that just felt dumb. Why wasn't I smart like the other kids? Why did spelling and reading come so hard to me? I remember a time when I was in high school, and my English teacher was making us read out loud (something that to this day still gives me panic attacks). As I started reading, I remember hearing a boy in the class say, "Oh my, *she* is reading. This is going to take *forever*." That same year I had an amazing teacher pull me aside. She took an interest in my education and decided to do some testing to see if I had a learning disability. Sure enough, she was right. I tested off the charts for having dyslexia. Dyslexia means that my brain doesn't retain a lot of the things I read and hear. I learned that

I learn best by doing, feeling and experiencing. It also means that I have to try a little harder than most when it comes to day-to-day reading, spelling and writing. I'm so thankful that God made me different from other people around me. I have learned to use my gifts and build a life I'm proud of. I no longer compare myself to those "smart" girls around me because I'm just as "smart" as them. I just have different talents!

Melody

There was a time in high school when my family wanted me to attend a boarding school in New York. They wanted me there for wonderful opportunities. It was a beautiful, fancy place. I went because I knew it was important to try, and I wanted to please my family. After only a month of being there, I knew that wasn't where I was supposed to be. However, after that long plane ride home to California, I didn't run into open arms like I thought I would. After a little while a cousin that I hardly knew, took me into her home and gave me the love, support, and encouragement I so desperately needed. After two years, she felt I was ready to be on my own. I was scared to leave and didn't have a local job, or another place to live, or much money in my bank account (girls, please, save your money!).

Then one day, very shortly after I knew I had to move out, my best friend and I stopped by a friend's house on the way to a college Bible study. The friend was a girl I grew up with in church! And she happened to be moving out of her condo that month! It was an instant decision to find a place to live together, and she even offered to help pay my half for the down payment to rent the house, wherever that would be. I was so excited!! Then off to Bible study we went. There, the friend that I drove with, wanted to have the group pray for me to help find a place to live and a job.

It was amazing! That night, another woman in the study came up to me and said that she was the apartment manager of some townhouses in my city! She told me to apply, and within a week, my friend and I had a place to live! Talk about an immediate answer to prayer.

Once we moved in, I was really hoping to find a job closer to my new house. Shortly after we got settled, I got a phone call from a guy that was at that Bible study. He said there was a job opening at his work that happened to be down the street from where I was living! I went in for an interview for one department of the business but when I showed up that position was no longer available! I was crestfallen, but then they told me there was another position open in another department and that I was hired for it!

And *there*, sweet girls, in that place, is where I met my amazing future husband, who later became a Christian, and an awesome dad to our kiddos.

So, as you can see, there were a lot of trials I went through. In some of them I was listening to God and in some of them I wasn't. But He worked all those things together for me because He loves me.

Caitlin

lesson six

Sheep with a Shepherd (baaa!)

Sheep with a Shepherd (baaa!)

Week 6- Layout

My sheep listen to my voice: I know
them, and they follow me.
John 10:27 (NIV)

Warm Up

Welcome the girls and give them stickers in their charts as earned.

Activity/Story/Discussion

Follow the Voice challenge

Have the girls choose a partner. One will be blind-folded, and the other will be the 'caller' who gives instructions. On 'go', the callers instruct the blind-folded partner as they go through a series of obstacles to get to an object. They must retrieve the object (color specific) and bring it back to the caller. All callers are speaking at the same time, forcing the blind-folded girls to listen carefully to their partner's voice. The point is to have them experience outside distractions and to stress the importance of tuning in to just one voice that will give them the right instructions. Once they've completed the activity, bring them in to your meeting space.

Main Idea

God loves us like a *protective* shepherd (John 10:14–15). Our job is to *listen* for His voice and *follow* it (John 10:3–5).

Fill in the blanks and look up the verses that support the idea.

Go to **tanyaschulz.com/whitestone** for free printable worksheets.

Discuss

1. What do you think a shepherd does?
2. What are sheep like? How do they feel about their shepherd?
3. How is God like a shepherd?
4. If we are His sheep, how should we behave?
5. How do we recognize His voice?

Guess the Voice game

Have the girls listen to the pre-recorded voices of their parents and each other saying the same phrase, "I love you. Have a great night!" and have them guess which voice belongs to whom.

Sword Drill

Play the books of the Bible song, then look up the scriptures below. Make it more challenging for the girls who are consistently the fastest, by hiding their Bibles ahead of time
Psalm 100:3
Ezekiel 34:11–12

John 10:3–5
Isaiah 40:11
John 10:14–15

Prayer Time

Each girl is invited to share a request, and the requests are divided among the girls to be prayed over together

Wrap Up

Make it Real …

The challenge for this week is to either:

1. Find a verse about being a sheep or about God being our shepherd, and share it next week, or
2. Watch for a time when you feel God is protecting you like a loving shepherd this week, then share it with the group.

Hide It in Your Heart

Have the girls write out their memory verse for the week.

Supplies needed:

blindfolds
simple obstacle course set up
colored objects to retrieve
prerecorded voices of the parents and girls, saying "I love you. Have a great night!" (collect ahead of time)
snacks
pens for fill in the blanks
a Bible for each girl

Sheep with a Shepherd (baaa!)

My sheep listen to my voice; I know
them, and they follow me.
John 10:27 (NIV)

Main Idea

God loves us like a _____ shepherd
(John 10:14—15). Our job is to _____ for
His voice and _____ it (John 10:3—5).

Think About It?

1. What do you think a shepherd does?
2. What are sheep like? How do they feel about their shepherd?
3. How is God like a shepherd?
4. If we are His sheep, how should we behave?
5. How do we recognize His voice?

Make it Real!

The challenge for this week is to either:

1. Find a verse about being a sheep or about God being our
   shepherd, and share it next week ... or,
2. Tell us about a time when you felt God protected you like a
   loving shepherd this week.

Hidin' it in my heart ...

lesson seven

Takin' it in ... Pourin' it out

Takin' it in Pourin' it out

Do not merely listen to the word, and so
deceive yourselves. Do what it says.
James 1:22 (NIV)

Warm Up

Welcome the girls and give them stickers in their charts as
earned.

Activity/Story/Discussion

Main Idea

Read the Bible and *do what it says!*
Fill your heart to **OVERFLOWING** with His Word
and His love ... then see where it *splashes!*

Fill in the blanks and look up the verses that support the idea.

Go to **tanyaschulz.com/whitestone** for free printable
worksheets.

Activity

Take the girls outside and circle up around a table. Pour water into a tall cup and say that the cup represents you, and the water represents God's Word, Christian music, prayer, and surrounding yourself with godly people. Then use that tall cup to pour water into other smaller cups, saying this represents you, using what you've learned to bless others. You are 'pouring' into their lives. The problem comes when you've used up all your 'water'. If you're not constantly refilling your cup, you won't have anything to pour out.

Next, pull out the hose and run it into a cup that sits on top of a pyramid of other cups, letting it overflow until all the other cups are full and overflowing. Explain that when we are constantly in God's Word, praying, listening to Christian music and surrounding ourselves with godly people, we can continually pour into the lives around us.

Story

Zoey and Summer ~ Actions Speak Louder than Words

Discuss

1. Was the Bible only written for people in the olden days?
2. What does it mean to say the Bible is 'alive and active'?
3. How is reading the Bible daily, like filling up a cup to overflowing?
4. What might we "spill" over onto others?
5. Who might we spill onto, or splash?

Sword Drill

Play the books of the Bible song, then look up the scriptures below. Make it more challenging for the girls who are consistently the fastest, by hiding their Bibles ahead of time

Proverbs 22:17–18   John 13:34–35
1 John 4:19–21   Romans 5:5
Matthew 5:14–16   James 1:22–24

Prayer Time

Each girl is invited to share a prayer request and the requests are divided among the girls to be prayed over together.

Wrap Up

Make it Real

Choose one of the following verses to read every day this week. Find a way to make it real... *do it!*

Proverbs 21:23   Proverbs 14:23
Proverbs 20:19   Proverbs 21:14
Proverbs 15:30   Proverbs 19:20
Proverbs 22:9   Proverbs 15:1
Proverbs 20:22

Hide it in Your Heart

Have the girls write out their memory verse for the week

> Supplies needed:
>
> outside table
> hose
> tall cup
> a few small cups
> snacks
> pens for filling in the blanks
> a Bible for each girl

Takin' it in ...
Pourin' it out

Do not merely listen to the word, and so
deceive yourselves. DO WHAT IT SAYS.
James 1:22 (NIV)

Main Idea

Read the Bible and _____ _____
_____ _____! Fill your heart to
OVERFLOWING with His Word and His love
... then see where it _____:)

Think About It?

1. Was the Bible only written for people in the olden days?
2. What does it mean to say the Bible is 'alive and active'?
3. How is reading the Bible daily, like filling up a cup to overflowing?
4. What might we "spill" over onto others?
5. Who might we spill onto, or splash?

Make it Real!

Choose one of the following verses to read every day this week. Find a way to make it real (DO IT!!!).

Proverbs 21:23   Proverbs 15:30
Proverbs 20:19   Proverbs 22:9

Proverbs 20:22   Proverbs 19:20
Proverbs 14:23   Proverbs 15:1
Proverbs 21:14

Hidin' it in my heart ...

Zoey and Summer ~ Actions Speak Louder than Words!

Zoey and Summer were super excited, because their families were getting together for a picnic after church, and the parents wanted to tell them something special. The girls were imagining all the possibilities. Were they finally getting permission to go to summer camp together? Was Zoey allowed to get her ears pierced like she'd been begging for, for years? Was Summer going to get the puppy she'd dreamed of? The girls felt like Sunday afternoon would never come.

Church was great. Zoey and Summer loved their teacher and the chance to hear about Jesus from someone who truly loves Him. But they were a bit distracted. Finally, it was time to drive to the park for their picnic. It was agonizing listening to the dads talk about sports as they sloooowwwlly laid out the blankets and watching the moms so caaaarefully lay out the food. Get on with it already, they thought! It wasn't until the prayer was said and everyone had a plate of food in front of them, that Zoey burst out, "I can't stand it any longer! What's the special news you have for us?!?" The parents laughed, then looked at each other. Zoey's dad spoke up first. "Okay girls. We *do* have something to tell you, but first you need to solve a kind of riddle. We're going to tell you three stories. If you can figure out what the common theme is in the three stories, then we'll give you the news." The girls sat up straighter, ready for the stories and hopeful they could figure it out. Summer's mom told the first story.

There was a young man who was asked to housesit for a week while his aunt and uncle went away. He would be paid to live in the house and take care of the plants, feed the dog, and just watch over the place in general. The young man was eager to live on his own for the week and was confident it would be no problem. He arrived on a Sunday and his aunt handed him a piece of paper with instructions written very carefully on it. It said things like, feed Rover 1 ½ cups of dry dog food in the morning and the evening. Take him for a walk each day and please pick up his poop daily so the neighbor's cat doesn't eat it. Water my thirsty ferns three times a day because they sit in direct sunlight and will die if they aren't watered. Collect our mail every afternoon and put it in the box by the door. Please eat up the food I've left for you in the fridge, so it doesn't go bad. The young man read the list carefully, to be sure he didn't have any questions, and then waved good-bye to his aunt and uncle.

The week went by and the aunt and uncle were driving back after their time away. They were looking forward to coming home, until they reached the driveway. The first thing they saw was the overflowing mailbox. Envelopes were shoved inside until it was so packed, the letters spilled out onto the sidewalk. The wind must've carried some of them down the walk because there was a trail of mail almost to the neighbor's house. The aunt and uncle stepped out of their car and were met with a horrible stench in the air. Piles of dog poop filled their yard! They looked at each other with concern, thinking something must've happened to the young man, but just then, the front door opened and there he was—smiling a big hello to them. Everyone went inside and with one glance around, the aunt and uncle determined that the young man must've lost the instructions he was given a week back. All their ferns were dry and brown, and crumbled into pieces with barely a touch. The kitchen smelled rancid, and when the aunt opened the fridge door, she nearly fell over from the smell and sight of all the moldy rotten food inside. The uncle called for his beloved pet, but Rover never came. He lay dead in the bedroom, flies circling around his head. The aunt and uncle looked at the young man in horror and asked, "What happened???? Did you lose our instructions???" The young man replied, "No. I have them right here in my pocket. But after the third day I didn't even need to read them. I memorized them! Want to hear it? I can tell you word for word what you wrote." The aunt and uncle kicked him out of the house, along with the instructions he had memorized. Needless to say, he didn't get paid.'

Zoey and Summer felt a bit sick to their stomach at the thought of the dead dog. They didn't quite understand how the young man could've messed up so badly if he did, indeed, read all the instructions.

Zoey's mom cleared her throat and said, "Ready for your next story girls?" They nodded, so she began.

This story is about a girl named Lucy. Lucy is twelve years old and has long curly brown hair and milky white skin. She is confident and well-liked by her peers. One morning, in the middle of the week, she woke up and stretched, looking forward to her day. She got out of bed and pulled up the covers, arranging her pillows and stuffed animals exactly how she wanted them for the day. She zipped to the bathroom to go potty, and when she stood in front of the sink to wash her hands, she looked up at the mirror with a shriek! What she saw shocked her! She must've drooled in her sleep and got her hair wet, because half of her hair was plastered to the side of her face, while the other half was matted and sticking up in all directions! She had spaghetti sauce from last night's meal, circling her mouth as if she'd tried to put orange lipstick on and missed by a mile. And to top things off, she had a huge zit on the tip of her nose! She was embarrassed to look at herself, never mind go to school like this. Lucy washed her hands and went back to her room to get dressed. When she came to the table for breakfast with her family, everyone stared at her in horror. Where was well-put-together Lucy? And why didn't she fix her hair, wash her face and somehow cover up that zit?? They had to leave for school in five minutes. Despite what Lucy saw in the mirror, she went to school looking that way ... and got a LOT of stares!

Summer giggled and said, "On a day like that, I'd be thankful I'm home schooled!" Zoey said, "Yeah, but why on earth wouldn't she *do* anything about it?"

Summer's dad stepped up next and said, "Okay girls, here's the last one. See if you can find any similarities in these stories that you can link to a common theme."

A dad, just like me, was sitting in his living room reading the newspaper on a Saturday morning, when his ten-year old daughter Carrie bounced down the stairs. "Dad," she started. "I'm bored. I have nothing to do and no one to play with." Her dad put down the paper and looked at her with a smile. "I'll tell you what. I have no plans today. If you go upstairs and clean your room, we can go to the mall and then out for ice cream together." Carried loved this idea! She ran up the stairs to her room, two at a time, and closed the door behind her. Twenty minutes later she came downstairs and declared she was ready to go. Her dad said, "Let's see how you did on your room. If it's all cleaned up, we'll go." He went upstairs and into her room but turned around in a hurry. "Uh, Carrie. Didn't you understand what I asked you to do?" Carrie said, "Yes. You said ... and I quote ... If you go upstairs and clean your room, we can go to the mall and then out for ice cream together." The dad looked at Carrie for a minute, thinking she would say something more. Maybe something that would explain why her room still looked like a tornado hit it. But she said nothing more. "Let's try this again Carrie. I won't take you to the mall or to ice cream until your room is clean. Got it?" "Got it," declared Carrie as she rushed back into her room.

Thirty minutes later, Carrie found her dad in the kitchen, drinking a cup of coffee. She handed him a piece of paper that had the title 'Clean your room' at the top. Below it she had neatly written the phrase clean your room in five different languages, plus she had written out the definition of each word. She stood there proudly while he looked it over. When his eyes lifted to hers, they looked a little confused. He walked past her and headed to her room yet again, only to find it looked exactly the same, except with her lap top computer open on her bed. "Carrie, I asked you to CLEAN YOUR ROOM, not tell me how to say it in Greek, Latin, Hebrew, French and Spanish! The definitions mean nothing to me. Now, we're cutting into our time at the mall. I'm serious about this." Carrie sighed and returned to her room while her dad returned to his coffee.

It was another 40 minutes before her dad came to check out her room for the third time. Before he could utter a word, Carrie launched into a full script she had typed out. She began, "If I cleaned my room, this is how I would do it and this is what it would look like when I was done." She handed him two pages—one with a list of possible ways to clean and organize her room, and one with a sketch of the clean room once it was done. Clearly, she had done her research and put a lot of time into thinking about cleaning her room. The room, however, was unchanged. Carrie never did get to go to the mall or have ice cream with her dad.

Summer and Zoey thought this story was absurd. Who, in their right mind, would spend so much time thinking about how to do something without actually *doing* something? They didn't want to say it out loud, but both of them were thinking this Carrie girl was pretty stupid.

Zoey's dad presented the challenge again. "Zoey and Summer, I'll give you two minutes to talk it over, and then you need to tell us what the common theme is for these three stories. If you are correct, then we'll tell you the special news." The girls turned toward each other and whispered their thoughts before agreeing on their final answer. Zoey nudged Summer to do the talking, so she spoke up for the both of them. "In every story, the main character was given some information they had to *do* something about, but they never followed through. The young man was given written instructions but ignored them.

Lucy learned from looking in the mirror but didn't change her appearance. And Carrie was told what to do, but never actually *did* what she was told! We think the common theme is that actions speak louder than words ... and these people just used words." The four parents clapped and cheered at this answer, making it clear that the girls were correct. "Well done girls!" Zoey's dad continued. "That's exactly right. In James 1:22 (NIV) it says, 'Do not merely listen to the Word and so deceive yourselves. Do what it says.' The four of us have been talking about how proud we are of you two. You've been reading your Bibles almost every day. But more importantly, you've been applying it to your life, showing love to people around you and honoring Jesus in the way you live. We'd like to reward you ... with a trip to Disneyland!"

The girls squealed in delight, jumping up and down together in their excitement. They had gone through some ups and downs that year and had learned a lot about how God wanted them to respond, but they never imagined getting this special reward. It was going to be a great summer!

THE END.

lesson eight

Open for Cleaning

*O*pen for Cleaning

Week 8- Layout

The light of the righteous shines brightly, but
the lamp of the wicked is snuffed out.
Proverbs 13:9 (NIV)

Warm Up

Welcome the girls and give them stickers in their charts as
earned.

Activity/ Story/ Discussion

Main Idea

Invite God to *clean* every corner of your life, so
that you may *shine* His light more brightly!

Fill in the blanks and look up the verses that support the idea.

Go to **tanyaschulz.com/whitestone** for free printable
worksheets.

Activity

Take the girls outside and circle up around a table. Each will have a dirty jar and lid to clean, along with the cleaning supplies to scrub and shine them well. They will also be given a tea light.

Tell the girls that this jar represents them, and that in order to shine Jesus' light brightly to those around us (be attractive because of His love in us), we need to ask Jesus to clean any areas that don't allow the light through. Have them clean their jars while you tell the story, and then place their tea lights inside and see how well they shine through the clean glass.

Story

Zoey and Summer - Let your Light Shine!

Discuss

1. What kind of 'dirt' might a person have in his/her life? *(Use poster board to make a list together under the title, "DIRT in my life" Ideas might be: gossip, lying, hate, coveting, disobeying, greed, cheating, swearing, being disrespectful/talking back, etc.)*
2. How do you get rid of this dirt?
3. Once God has forgiven you, and washed away the dirt, making you clean, will that dirt ever come back?
4. How do we keep ourselves clean and shiny?
5. What does it mean to let your light shine? Why do we care if we shine?

Sword Drill

Play the books of the Bible song, then look up the scriptures below. Make it more challenging for the girls who are consistently the fastest, by hiding their Bibles ahead of time

Matthew 23:25–26   Hebrews 10:22
Matthew 5:16   Daniel 12:3
Philippians 2:14–15   Proverbs 13:9

Prayer Time

Each girl is invited to share a prayer request, and the requests are divided among the girls to be prayed over together.

Wrap Up

Make it Real

<u>Get alone with Jesus</u> this week (in your room, outside on a swing, or wherever you're alone), and ask Him to show you the 'dirt' in your life. When you think you know what it is, ask Him to make you clean so that you'll shine more brightly.

Hide it in Your Heart

Have the girls write out their memory verse for the week.

Supplies needed:

outside table(s)
small jars and lids you've made dirty
cleaning supplies to share (a toothbrush each, water, dish soap, rags/towels)
tea lights for each girl
poster board
marker
snacks
pens for filling in the blanks
a Bible for each girl

Open for Cleaning

The light of the righteous shines brightly, but
the lamp of the wicked is snuffed out.
Proverbs 13:9 (NIV)

Main Idea

Invite God to _____
every corner of your life, so that you may
_____ His light more brightly!

Think About It?

1.   What kind of 'dirt' might a person have in his/her life?
2.   How do you get rid of that dirt?
3.   Once God has forgiven you, and washed away the dirt, making you clean, will that dirt ever come back?
4.   How do we keep ourselves clean and shiny?
5.   What does it mean to let your light shine? Why do we care if we shine?

Make it Real!

Get alone with Jesus this week (in your room, outside on a swing, or wherever you're alone), and ask Him to show you the 'dirt' in your life. When you think you know what it is, ask Him to make you clean so that you'll shine more brightly.

Hidin' it in my heart ...

Zoey and Summer ~ Let Your Light Shine!

Disneyland was incredible! The girls were talking about their favorite rides and shows for days after they came home. The next big event of the summer was Camp Zoolia, and although it didn't involve the same excitement as Disneyland did, the girls very much looked forward to it. This year's theme was 'Let your Light Shine'. Neither Zoey nor Summer knew what that meant, exactly, but they would find out at the camp kick off on Sunday.

There were a lot of hyper kids with ice cream in their bellies Sunday night, but when the whistle blew, they knew to gather around so they could learn more about the theme of camp. Zoey and Summer watched intently as the director pulled out a nasty dirty glass jar. He lifted it up high for all the kids and parents to see, then said, "Tonight, when the sun goes down and it gets dark outside, I want to light a candle and put it inside this glass jar so I can see a little better. But there's one problem. My jar is so filthy, I don't think my candlelight will shine very brightly. What can I do to fix this?" The kids shouted out, "Get a bigger candle!" and "Get a different jar!" and "Clean the jar!" The director went on to say, "This is like real life, you guys. This jar represents me, or you. The candle represents Jesus' light. We all have dirt that needs to be cleaned out of our lives so Jesus' light can shine more brightly through us. This week I want you to pray that God will show you what your dirt is—stuff like lying or being ungrateful—and then we'll pray together for God to wash you clean. Understood?" Everyone yelled in unison, "Understood!"

The next day the beach was invaded by Zoey, Summer and their Camp Zoolia friends. It was a super fun day in the sun except that Sally came. Zoey got along with most people, but she really, strongly disliked Sally. She would say she hated Sally, but her mom said that word wasn't allowed in their family. All afternoon Sally followed Zoey around, telling her what to do, criticizing her sand creations, tripping Zoey in line tag when the adults weren't watching and just driving her crazy! Zoey knew that if she told her mom what Sally was doing, her mom would tell her to ignore Sally, or just be nice. So instead, Zoey took Summer aside and vented, "Sally is such a *pest*. I can't stand her! Look at her, standing there all smug, as if she's better than everyone else. Arghh!" Zoey stared harshly at Sally while whispering her frustration to Summer, and silently wished a giant fish would jump out of the ocean and swallow Sally up. It may have been a beautiful day, but Zoey felt anything but "sunny" on the inside, and she was actually glad when it was time to go home.

Summer had to miss the hike on Tuesday, but that was okay. Her favorite activity of the week was game day. She chose her favorite shorts and tank top, then picked out a matching headband and flip flops. She wasn't totally a fashion girl, but she did appreciate a well put-together outfit, and this was one of them. Secretly she wondered how many compliments she'd get today. As her mom drove her to the park, Summer looked out the window hoping for a head start on seeing who was already at game day. As soon as the park was in view, she saw Millie Parker—one of her closest friends from church. Millie was super nice and a really good athlete. In fact, thought Summer, I'll be sure to pick her as my partner if we need to pair up for game day. That would be a huge advantage! Summer could see that Millie was wearing something with zebra print on it, but she couldn't quite make it out from this distance. Her mom parked the car and Summer practically bolted out her door, eager to see her friends and get on with game day. Zoey arrived at the same time, so the girls raced to the field together. Millie met up with them, smiling from ear to ear. Now Summer could see Millie's outfit ... every adorable piece of it. She had zebra print ankle length pants, a black tank top, and dangly earrings in the shape of little zebras. Her hair was pulled up in a high pony-tail so the earrings really stood out. The whole look was amazing—athletic *and* fashionable! All of a sudden Summer didn't feel so good about the outfit she'd chosen for herself that morning. Compared to Millie, she felt out of style and not at all athletic. She silently wished she could switch closets with Millie … maybe even lives. The more she thought about it, the more she began to believe Millie had a better life all around. She was pretty and confident, athletic and smart, had nice clothes, her ears pierced *and* a super cool bedroom in a two-story house with an art wall where she could paint and repaint whatever she wanted.

Zoey waved her hand in front of Summer's eyes. "Earth to Summer!" Summer blinked, returning to reality. She must've been staring into space. Time to focus! She tried to convince herself it didn't matter what she wore, but all throughout game day she couldn't help but wish she had what Millie had. A perfect life.

The wrap up barbecue came faster than anyone wanted it to. Camp Zoolia was coming to a close and the director was inviting all the kids to gather around the campfire for one final assignment. "At the beginning of the week I asked you to invite God to open your eyes to the dirt in your life. I want you to think about that now. Once you have something or some things in mind, ask God to forgive you and wipe you clean. Imagine him scrubbing out that dirt!" Zoey's first thought was that Sally would have no trouble with this assignment since she had a *lot* of dirt. She was mean and judgmental and not very Christ-like at all. Just as soon as those thoughts came into Zoey's head, she had another thought. She too, had a big dirt pile in her life. A pile of hate. Yes, Sally was a pest, but Zoey needed to choose to show love to her, instead of hate. She bowed her head and began to pray.

Summer sat for a long time, unsure what dirt she needed washed away. She knew she wasn't perfect, but nothing stood out, until her eyes met with Millie's. They smiled at each other and then Summer remembered how consumed she was with wanting Millie's life. There was a word for that. Not jealousy, but ... Summer thought back to the list of 'dirt' they came up with as a group, trying to recall the word. Covet. That was it. It means to want something someone else has. And it's a sin. Summer closed her eyes and asked Jesus to forgive her for coveting Millie's life and not being grateful for her own. She asked Him to wipe her clean and give her a fresh start.

The girls lifted their heads at the same time, their eyes shining a little more brightly. They were ready to go back into their worlds and let their lights SHINE!

THE END.

lesson nine

New Creations

New Creations

Therefore, if anyone is in Christ, the new creation has come:
the old has gone, the new is here!
2 Corinthians 5:17 (NIV)

Warm Up

Welcome the girls and give them stickers in their charts as earned.

Activity/ Story/ Discussion

Main Idea

When we invite Jesus into our lives, He takes the *old* me and makes a *new* me! Everyone has *potential* to be made new, and we are all *works* in progress.

Fill in the blanks and look up the verses that support the idea.

Go to **tanyaschulz.com/whitestone** for free printable worksheets.

Pick a Station

The girls will be divided into groups and sent to one of the following stations. Once they've completed the station, or a time limit has been reached, they will move on to another station.

Station one: Create a Jean Purse
Take a pair of old jeans and 'upcycle' them into a jean purse! The girls will follow the D.I.Y. instructions provided and will work with a leader to sew a purse, then add their first initials to claim it as their own. Explain as you go, that although the jeans are the same, they are being made new – given a new purpose and look. This is just what Jesus does for us. He takes something old and makes something new, with a new purpose and 'look'. We will be different with Jesus in our hearts!

Station two: New Creation Station
Go to **tanyaschulz.com/whitestone** for free printable worsksheets
Fill in the worksheet, provided, and answer questions that are personal. Look up scriptures to find God's perspective on being made new and find out how we should view those who are a 'work in progress'.

Station three: Snack Table
Enjoy a snack while you wait

Station four: Play Outside
Play outside while you wait

Sword Drill

No sword drill today.

Prayer Time

Each girl is invited to share a prayer request, and the requests are divided among the girls to be prayed over together.

Wrap Up

Make it Real

Interview someone who became a Christian later in their life and ask them how they are different since asking Jesus to be in their lives. Come back next week and tell us who you talked to and what they said.

Hide it in Your Heart

Have the girls write out their memory verse for the week.

Supplies needed:

old jeans (a pair for each girl)
a fabric initial for each girl
sewing supplies (sewing machine, thread, fabric scissors, iron, needle for hand stitching, lots of patience!)
the pattern/plan (see D.I.Y. page)
copies of the New Creation Scenarios
snacks
pens for fill in the blanks and New Creation Station
a Bible for them to share

New Creations

Therefore, if anyone is in Christ, the new creation
has come: the old has gone, the new is here!
2 Corinthians 5:17 (NIV)

Main Idea

When we invite Jesus into our lives, He takes
the _____ me and makes a _____ me!
Everyone has _____ to be made new,
and we are all a _____ in progress.

Think About It?

1. What does it mean to 'upcycle' something?
2. Can you imagine something ugly becoming something beautiful? Do you see the potential in things or people?
3. How can we show patience to those people who are a 'work in progress'?
4. How can we say thank you to Jesus for having patience with *us* as He does His work in our own lives?

Make it Real!

Interview someone who became a Christian later in their life and ask them how they are different since asking Jesus to be in their lives. Come back next week and tell us who you talked to and what they said.

Hidin' it in my heart ...

New Creation Station!

Scenario #1
Zoey has always had a hard time loving Sally. They have been put together in a small group at church, so now they have to work together on projects *every* Sunday. Zoey knows that Sally just accepted Jesus into her heart six months ago, and that no one in her family goes to church except her aunt, who brings Sally each week. Zoey's Sunday School teacher takes Zoey aside and asks her to look up **Proverbs 15:18** and apply it to her life when she's working with Sally. What is she asking Zoey to do???

Scenario #2
Summer used to have a problem with lying. She didn't mean to do it ... it just came out! When she became a Christian, God came alongside of her and helped her become aware of this problem, but there were still times when Summer struggled. Last Saturday she was invited to go shopping with Millie, a friend from church. They had a great time and even got matching outfits in their favorite colors. When Zoey saw Summer at church the next day, she said, "Wow! You look so cute! Is that a new outfit?" Summer didn't want Zoey to feel badly that she had gone shopping with Millie, so she tried to make it no big deal and said, "No, it's just something I haven't worn for a while. How are you?" The outfit seemed to be forgotten until Millie walked in, wearing the exact same outfit. Zoey gave Summer a puzzled look, then turned away. Read **Ephesians 4:20–25**. What does Summer need to do?

Scenario #3
You have been faithful to the Whitestone Girls Club and are learning what it means to live for Jesus in your every-day life. You have done *so* well on your chart and have almost a perfect record of stickers! Unfortunately, you get sick and have to miss a week. You have the assignment and the verse

to memorize, but you just don't get around to reading it or doing it! Our meeting night rolls around, and you feel guilty for not being ready. You know you won't get a sticker for your verse or your assignment this week and you're super bummed about it. You think to yourself, "I should just quit. Everyone else probably did their homework. I'll never catch up, so what's the point." Your mom senses your discouragement and tells you to look up **2 Corinthians 4:16–18**. What two things is she asking of you?

To not …

To fix your eyes on…

Two more things to do before you move on to the next station …

1. Write out a **'thank you' to Jesus** for being patient with you as He works in your life, making you the girl He plans for you to be.
2. Go find your worksheet and **write out your scripture** on the bottom of the page (as we always do).

D.I.Y. Fashion Jeans Bag

Find an old pair of jeans that you love, and 'upcycle' them into a purse with awesome pockets!

1. Lay the jeans flat and cut to the length you want for your bag (cut 1 leg first, then match up with the other leg).

2. Cut along the crotch seam on both sides, to remove bulk.

3. Turn it inside out and fold with the crease on the front.

4. Sew straight down on the sides so it takes on a rectangle shape (sew UNDER the zipper).

5. Cut off excess material and refold front ways.

6. Sew across the bottom.

7. Pull the corners to a point and stitch across (do NOT cut off excess).

8. Cut the purse strap(s) from the leg material. Double the material and sew right side to right side.

9. Turn it right side out and you'll have your strap.

10. Choose the inside lining & cut to the same shape as the bag.

11. Attach strap to inside of jean material.

12. Stitch lining (inside out) then hand stitch the lining to the inside ... except the bottom corners, which will be machine stitched.

13. When stitching corners together, inside out to inside out, then all of it turns right side out together.

14. Attach any embellishments (ie. your first initial).

15. Fill it up and use it with pride!

lesson ten

Extraordinary!

Extraordinary!

Because we know that this extraordinary day is just ahead, we pray for you all the time—pray that our God will make you fit for what He's called you to be, pray that He'll fill your good ideas and acts of faith with His own energy so that it all amounts to something. If your life honors the name of Jesus, He will honor you. Grace is behind and through all of this, our God giving Himself freely, the Master, Jesus Christ, giving Himself freely.
2 Thessalonians 1:11–12 (the Message)

Warm Up

Welcome the girls and give them the final stickers in their charts as earned. Determine the prize value!

Activity/ Story/ Discussion

Main Idea

I, *Tanya*, am called to be extraordinary! God will *equip* me to make a difference for Him. No *risks* means no *rewards*. Trust God and live *confidently*!

Fill in the blanks.

Go to **tanyaschulz.com/whitestone** for free printable worksheets.

Review

What is a Whitestone girl?

We are ...
Women in the making, girls for now.
Here for a purpose.
In it to win it.
Truly beautiful, and fruity.
Eating flour, picturing cake.
Sheep with a Shepherd.
Taking it in, pouring it out.
Open for cleaning.
New creations.
EXTRAORDINARY!!!

Object lesson

Set up a balance beam in an open space, and have the girls sit and watch you as you act out the story. Tell it in the first or third person. If you are unable to find a balance beam, use a curb, or lay a rope across the ground, or stick a long row of tape on your carpet floor, and pretend it's a balance beam!

(start by standing on the beam)

There is a lot we've learned about Jesus, the Bible, and how we are to live as Christians, but there is also a lot we *don't* understand. Sometimes bad things happen in our lives—even after we've asked Jesus into our hearts. Maybe someone we love dies, or a friend decides to turn her back on you, or we get really sick or hurt, or we feel sad or lonely, or things just don't go like we want them to.

(slowly go down to your knees and hands, then eventually on your belly so you're holding on tightly to the beam)

So, we choose to be safe and kind of just keep to ourselves. We surround ourselves with only people who are like us—just Christians that go to the same church. We sit in the same spot every Sunday at church and talk to the same people. We don't talk to our neighbors because they might listen to bad music or use swear words and we just wouldn't know what to say. We help others when we're asked to, but we don't offer, because you never know how the other person will feel about being helped and you don't want to offend anyone. We stay away from kids at school who are mean or rude, and don't join any extra activities just in case we have to talk about our faith. We stay quiet when we hear people questioning if God is real because we don't want to say the wrong thing. We pray that we'll always be healthy and that our grandmas and grandpas will just die in their sleep so they don't have to have any pain ... and say "that would be nice for me too."

(slowly release yourself from the beam and do an exaggerated finish with a bow)

And then we die and stand before the judge. Imagine you're before the judge in gymnastics after a routine like I just did. Is the judge going to stand and clap and give me a good score? Lots of Christians want to be safe so they don't fall—so they don't make a mistake or look foolish. Then one day they'll stand before the Judge (God). Will He say "Well done?" The majority of Christians may be okay with this safe ordinary life. But I want to live confidently. I want to do bold things for Jesus. And if I fall, that's okay. I'll get back up and try again. I want to be extraordinary for Jesus so that one day I'll stand before Him and He'll say, "Well done."

Discuss

1. Which routine do you think would impress the Judge? An ordinary one with no falling, or an extraordinary one with a few mistakes?
2. What makes up a 'good routine' in real life?
3. Does living an extraordinary life mean you are *always* bold?
4. What will make *your* routine unique?
5. Decide for yourself – do you want an ordinary life, or an extraordinary one?

Special Send Off

Decorate the kitchen or a special space with little white lights strung around the ceiling. Set up a table with a fancy napkin at each girl's spot, a mini bottle of sparkling juice, a glittery ring (fake, of course), and a personal letter from you to them, saying why you think each girl is extraordinary. Have a celebratory cake for finishing Whitestone girls and talk about the highlights from the study.

Pray for each other, finishing with a prayer for each of us to live extraordinary lives for Jesus. Have them write in each other's binders, saying one thing they think is extraordinary about the others.

Decide if you want to do a reunion party down the road, and announce it if you choose!

Supplies needed:

balance beam (or a 2x4 board supported by bricks, or a rope!)
little white lights
fancy napkins
mini sparkling apple juice bottles
fake glittery rings for each girl
a personal note for each girl
special dessert
colored pens to write in their binders

$\mathcal{E}$xtraordinary!

Because we know that this **extraordinary** day is just
ahead, we pray for you all the time—pray that our God
will make you fit for what He's called you to be, pray
that He'll fill your good ideas and acts of faith with His
own energy so that it all amounts to something.
<u>If your life honors the name of Jesus, He will
honor you.</u> Grace is behind and through all of
this, our God giving Himself freely, the Master,
Jesus Christ, giving Himself freely.
2 Thessalonians 1:11–12 (the Message)

Main Idea

I, _____, am called to be
extraordinary! God will _____
me to make a difference for Him. No
_____ means no _____.
Trust God and live _____!

What makes me extraordinary ... according to my friends?

Congratulations!

You have completed the 10-week
Whitestone Girls Study!
I can't wait to celebrate with
you all soon. I LOVE YOU.

You did it! I'm so proud of you for taking the time to invest in these young ladies' lives. It was time well spent, and although you may not see the dividends now, maybe one day you'll be blessed to see a glimpse of what God has done to prepare their hearts for what's ahead.

One last note. I took photos each week that we met together, and after our ten weeks were over, I compiled the photos, and created mini photo albums for the girls with a few photos from each week. On the last page of their album, I listed some highlights from our time together, making sure I specifically named each girl at least once. We went out for ice cream and I presented them with their own album. It wasn't costly, and it was meaningful.

I would love to hear about your Whitestone girls adventure! Please go to my website: tanyaschulz.com and leave me a note or drop in a photo.

So happy to share this with you,

Tanya Schulz

Printed in the United States
By Bookmasters